A Literature Kit™ FOR

Loser

• • • • • • • • • • • • • • • • •

By Jerry Spinelli

Written by Nat Reed

GRADES 5 – 6

Classroom Complete Press

P.O. Box 19729
San Diego, CA 92159
Tel: 1-800-663-3609 | Fax: 1-800-663-3608
Email: service@classroomcompletepress.com

www.classroomcompletepress.com

ISBN-13: 978-1-55319-432-3
ISBN-10: 1-55319-432-2

© 2008

Permission to Reproduce

Critical Thinking Skills

Loser

Skills For Critical Thinking		1-4	5-7	8-9	10-11	12-14	15-17	18-20	21-23	24-26	27-30	Writing Tasks	Graphic Organizers
LEVEL 1 Knowledge	• Identify Story Elements	✓	✓	✓	✓	✓	✓	✓	✓	✓	✓	✓	✓
	• Recall Details	✓	✓	✓	✓	✓	✓	✓	✓	✓	✓	✓	✓
	• Match			✓	✓	✓	✓	✓	✓	✓	✓		✓
	• Sequence			✓			✓				✓		✓
LEVEL 2 Comprehension	• Compare and Contrast	✓	✓				✓		✓	✓		✓	✓
	• Summarize	✓	✓	✓	✓	✓	✓	✓	✓		✓	✓	✓
	• State Main Idea						✓					✓	✓
	• Describe	✓	✓	✓	✓	✓	✓					✓	✓
	• Classify	✓						✓		✓			
LEVEL 3 Application	• Plan			✓				✓	✓		✓	✓	✓
	• Interview		✓			✓		✓				✓	
	• Infer Outcomes	✓	✓					✓	✓	✓	✓	✓	
LEVEL 4 Analysis	• Draw Conclusions	✓	✓	✓	✓	✓	✓	✓		✓	✓	✓	✓
	• Identify Supporting Evidence		✓		✓		✓		✓	✓		✓	
	• Infer Character Motivations		✓	✓	✓		✓	✓	✓	✓		✓	
	• Identify Cause & Effect			✓			✓		✓		✓		✓
LEVEL 5 Synthesis	• Predict	✓	✓		✓	✓	✓		✓		✓	✓	
	• Design			✓	✓							✓	✓
	• Create		✓			✓		✓				✓	
	• Write An Alternative Ending To		✓				✓			✓		✓	
LEVEL 6 Evaluation	• State and Defend An Opinion	✓	✓	✓	✓	✓	✓	✓	✓	✓		✓	✓
	• Make Judgements	✓	✓	✓	✓	✓	✓	✓	✓	✓		✓	✓

Chapter Questions spans columns 1-4 through 27-30.

Based on Bloom's Taxonomy

Contents

• • • • • • • • • • • • • •

FREE! 6 Bonus Activities!

3 EASY STEPS to receive your 6 Bonus Activities!
• Go to our website:
www.classroomcompletepress.com\bonus
• Click on item CC2511 – Loser
• Enter pass code CC2511D

Assessment Rubric

Loser

Student's Name: _____ Assignment: _____ Level: _____

	Level 1	Level 2	Level 3	Level 4
Comprehension of Novel • information and details relevant to focus	• Demonstrates a limited understanding of the novel	• Demonstrates a basic understanding of the novel	• Demonstrates a good understanding of the novel	• Demonstrates a thorough understanding of the novel
Content • information and details relevant to focus	• Elements incomplete; key details missing	• Some elements complete; details missing	• All required elements completed; key details contain some description	• All required elements completed; enough description for clarity
Style • effective word choice and originality • precise language	• Little variety in word choice. • Language vague and imprecise	• Some variety in word choice. • Language somewhat vague and imprecise	• Good variety in word choice. • Language precise and quite descriptive	• Writer's voice is apparent throughout. Excellent choice of words. Precise language.
Conventions • spelling, language, capitalization, punctuation	• Errors seriously interfere with the writer's purpose	• Repeated errors in mechanics and usage	• Some errors in convention	• Few errors in convention

STRENGTHS:

WEAKNESSES:

NEXT STEPS:

Teacher Guide

Our resource has been created for ease of use by both TEACHERS and STUDENTS alike.

Introduction

This study guide is designed to give the teacher a number of helpful ways of making the study of this novel a more enjoyable and profitable experience for the students. The guide features a number of useful and flexible components, from which the teacher can choose. It is not expected that all of the activities will be completed.

One advantage to this approach to the study of a novel is that the student can work at his/her own speed, and the teacher can assign activities, etc. which match the student's abilities.

The study guide generally divides the novel by chapter and features reading comprehension and vocabulary questions. Themes include friendship, conformity and peer pressure, self worth and accepting peoples who may be different. Loser provides a wealth of opportunity for classroom discussion because of the vivid portrayal of the main character, Zinkoff, his odd eccentricities, and for the most part, the wonderful way he has of accepting not only himself, but also everyone around him.

How Is Our Literature Kit™ Organized?

STUDENT HANDOUTS

Chapter Activities (*in the form of reproducible worksheets*) make up the majority of our resource. For each chapter or group of chapters there are BEFORE YOU READ activities and AFTER YOU READ activities.

- The BEFORE YOU READ activities prepare students for reading by setting a purpose for reading. They stimulate background knowledge and experience, and guide students to make connections between what they know and what they will learn. Important concepts and vocabulary from the chapter(s) are also presented.

- The AFTER YOU READ activities check students' comprehension and extend their learning. Students are asked to give thoughtful consideration of the text through creative and evaluative short-answer questions and journal prompts.

Six **Writing Tasks** and three **Graphic Organizers** are included to further develop students' critical thinking and writing skills, and analysis of the text. (*See page 6 for suggestions on using the Graphic Organizers.*) The **Assessment Rubric** (*page 4*) is a useful tool for evaluating students' responses to the Writing Tasks and Graphic Organizers.

PICTURE CUES

Our resource contains three main types of pages, each with a different purpose and use. A **Picture Cue** at the top of each page shows, at a glance, what the page is for.

 Teacher Guide
- Information and tools for the teacher

 Student Handout
- Reproducible worksheets and activities

 Easy Marking™ Answer Key
- Answers for student activities

EASY MARKING™ ANSWER KEY

Marking students' worksheets is fast and easy with our **Answer Key**. Answers are listed in columns – just line up the column with its corresponding worksheet, as shown, and see how every question matches up with its answer!

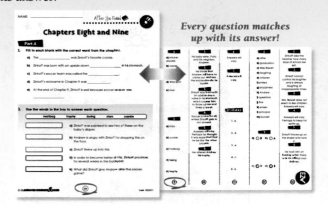

Every question matches up with its answer!

1,2,3
Graphic Organizer Transparencies

The three **Graphic Organizer Transparencies** included in our Literature Kit™ are especially suited to a study of **Loser**. Below are suggestions for using each organizer in your classroom, or they may be adapted to suit the individual needs of your students. The transparencies can be used on an overhead projector in teacher-led activities, and/or photocopied for use as student worksheets. To evaluate students' responses to any of the organizers, you may wish to use the **Assessment Rubric** (on page 4).

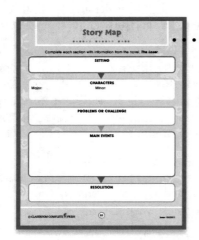

STORY MAP

Loser is an award-winning novel which vividly and sympathetically portrays its young protagonist, Zinkoff, and his journey through life from first grade to Middle School. Oblivious to his many physical and social shortcomings, he happily blunders through his early years, until finally his classmates begin to notice just how "different" he is. In the accompanying Story Map, students are asked to complete each section with details they learned from the novel; Setting (time and place); Major and Minor Characters; The Main Problem or Challenge faced by the main character; a brief Summary of the Plot; and the Resolution of the story. Found on Page 53.

COMPARING TWO CHARACTERS

Using a Venn Diagram, students are given the opportunity of comparing the main character, Zinkoff, with another character of their choice. They may choose another child for this (i.e. Hector Binn, Polly) or an adult (Zinkoff's dad, or one of his teachers). Students are asked to consider both physical characteristics and personality traits. Character traits shared by the two characters should go in the middle of the Venn Diagram.
Found on Page 54.

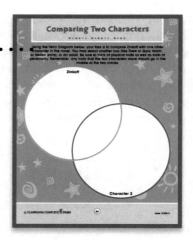

TIME LINE

Zinkoff's life is certainly filled with a number of unusual adventures and a good number of memorable characters (the "Oh Mailman Lady", Hector Binns, Miss Meeks, etc.). The students are expected to complete the Time Line by inserting at least a dozen major events from the novel. As a bonus activity the students can also be asked to identify the event that they consider to be the climax of the novel.
Found on Page 55.

Bloom's Taxonomy* for Reading Comprehension

The activities in our resource engage and build the full range of thinking skills that are essential for students' reading comprehension. Based on the six levels of thinking in Bloom's Taxonomy, questions are given that challenge students to not only recall what they have read, but move beyond this to understand the text through higher-order thinking. By using higher-order skills of application, analysis, synthesis and evaluation, students become active readers, drawing more meaning from the text, and applying and extending their learning in more sophisticated ways.

Our Literature Kit™, therefore, is an effective tool for any Language Arts program. Whether it is used in whole or in part, or adapted to meet individual student needs, our resource provides teachers with the important questions to ask, inspiring students' interest, creativity, and promoting meaningful learning.

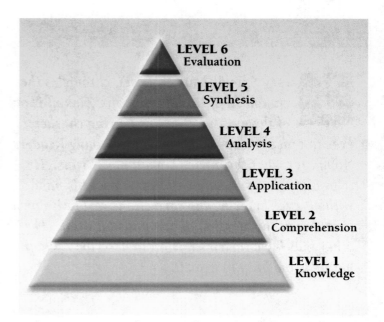

LEVEL 6
Evaluation

LEVEL 5
Synthesis

LEVEL 4
Analysis

LEVEL 3
Application

LEVEL 2
Comprehension

LEVEL 1
Knowledge

**BLOOM'S TAXONOMY:
6 LEVELS OF THINKING**

Bloom's Taxonomy is a widely used tool by educators for classifying learning objectives, and is based on the work of Benjamin Bloom.

Teaching Strategies — WHOLE-CLASS, SMALL GROUP AND INDEPENDENT STUDY

This novel can be approached in many ways. First, it can be tackled as a whole-class shared reading where all students have a copy of the text to follow along with as the teacher reads aloud. This provides for modeling of fluency and expression and makes the text accessible to all learners as the teacher supports students through the decoding and comprehension of the text.

The novel can also be used as one of several different books assigned to ability groups and read in a guided reading setting. The other novels could have similar themes or could be part of an author study. This way, all readers are reading text at their instructional level rather than being frustrated by inaccessible text.

The activities and questions provided in our Literature Kit™ can be used "as is" or modified to suit your needs. For example, the BEFORE YOU READ questions can be done as a whole class discussion, applying strategies such as "Think, Pair, Share" to

increase student participation and accountability.

Part A of the AFTER YOU READ activities can be used as a quick check for basic understanding and to inform the teacher about which students are in need of further support or remediation. Part B of the AFTER YOU READ activities provide more depth and challenge. Providing appropriate explicit teaching and scaffolding of the terms, elements and skills has occurred, students could complete Part B independently. Or, careful selection and reorganization of the activities could effectively meet the needs of small reading groups based upon reading strengths and needs.

Most importantly, regardless how teachers choose to implement these activities, modeling, direct instruction and the opportunity for guided practice before independent work is assigned is critical if student comprehension, performance and particularly enjoyment of reading is to be enhanced.

Summary of the Story

Jerry Spinelli's novel, Loser, chronicles the childhood of Donald Zinkoff. Zinkoff is one of the most unusual, endearing characters ever to grace the pages of a novel for Young Readers. No matter what the game, Zinkoff never wins. He trips over his own feet; constantly raises his hand without ever knowing the correct answer; falls down laughing at the mention of any unusual word. The other kids have their own word to describe Zinkoff, but he is too busy to hear it.

The novel traces Zinkoff's journey from first to sixth grade. It details his important friendships; marks his relationships with different teachers, and describes how he copes with various *shortcomings* that everyone but he and his parents deem terribly important.

Loser is an excellent novel which sensitively deals with the human spirit and the importance of failure. It is especially recommended for students struggling with acceptance among their peers, or who bear up under various negative labels.

Suggestions for Further Reading

OTHER BOOKS BY JERRY SPINELLI

The Bathwater Gang. 1990.
The Bathwater Gang Gets Down to Business. 1992.
Blue Ribbon Blues: A Tooter Tale. 1998.
Black Star, Bright Dawn. *Houghton Mifflin, 1988.*
Crash. 1996.
Do the Funky Pickle. 1992.
Dump Days. *Boston: 1988*
Fourth Grade Rats. 1991.
Jason and Marceline. 1986.
Knots in My Yo-Yo String. 1998.
The Library Card. 1997.

Maniac Magee. 1990.
Night of the Whale. 1985.
Picklemania. 1993.
School Daze. 1991.
Space Station Seventh Grade. 1982.
Stargirl. 2000.
There's a Girl in my Hammerlock. 1991.
Tooter Pepperday. 1995.
Who Put that Hair in My Toothbrush. 1984.
Wringer. 1997.

OTHER RECOMMENDED RESOURCES

My Sister Annie, *Bill Dodds,* © 1989
The Summer Kid, *Myrna Levy* © 1991
Reach for the Moon, *Samantha Abeel,* © 1997
Zipper, the Kid with ADHD, *C. Janover,* © 1977
He's My Brother, *Joe Lasker,* © 1974
Through Grandpa's Eyes, *Patricia MacLachlan,* ©1980
Trouble with School, *K & A Dunn,* ©1993
I'm the Big Sister Now, *M. Emmert,* ©1989
Be Good to Eddie Lee, *Virginia Fleming,* © 1993

Vocabulary

CHAPTERS 1 TO 4
• heedless • trolley • annoy • unpredictable • quiver • agreeable • instinct • remarkable • constraints • trudging • sift • giraffe • cubbyholes • alphabetical • atwitter

CHAPTERS 5 TO 7
• citizens • graduate • dramatically • crisply • confusion • represents • particular • confusion • disappointed • galloper • fascinated • apparently • congratulations • retread • comforters

CHAPTERS 8 TO 9
• acquires • Snickerdoodles • serious • pacifier • quilted • misinformed • announces • etiquette • haphazard • impressed • mailman • absolutely • intends • random • miraculously

CHAPTERS 10 TO 11
• annoying • untimely • intention • numerals • atrocious • apparent • clumsiness • antics • academic • mediocre • refrigerator • instructions • professional • pierces • pith

CHAPTERS 12 TO 14
• convalescing • descending • contrary • critical • distinct • solitary • reassures • urgent • immense • coarse • decaffeinated • consults • concerned • rainspouts • condemned

CHAPTERS 15 TO 17
• discoveries • grandly • independent • atrocious • orchestra • recital • stampede • anchor • pronounces • dashboard • rattletrap • payoff • visible • abundantly • mediocre

CHAPTERS 18 TO 20
• licorice • disconnect • exception • appoints • gaudy • blundering • embarrassed • housefronts • impression • ultimately • weave • assigned • congratulations • contribute • misspelling

CHAPTERS 21 TO 23
• gallop • cabinet • gooseberry • grimace • transparent • ghostlike • Olympics • circumstance • superintendent • galore • wince • boondocks • boisterous • diploma • frolic

CHAPTERS 24 TO 26
• asphalt • flurries • cafeteria • fragments • squirming • complained • alleyways • sprawls • silhouettes • staticky • crouched • Cleveland • waltzed • utterly • bluff

CHAPTER 27 TO 30
• spiral • canopy • dislodged • slogged • balmy • stashed • gaped • trance • delight • repeated • prickles • violently • icicle • confusion • description

Jerry Spinelli

Jerry Spinelli was born in Norristown, Pennsylvania. He attended Gettysburg College and John Hopkins University.

In 1991 he won the Newbery Award for his novel, *Maniac McGee* and in 1998 *Wringer* was named a Newbery Honor Book.

He and his wife, Eileen have six children and several grandchildren. Eileen Spinelli is Jerry's favorite author.

Jerry Spinelli's novels reflect the power of childhood memories and powerfully affect his work: "*Isn't it a magical, wonderful thing that our childhoods are not irretrievably lost to us, like the juice squeezed forever from an orange, and that without moving so much as an eyelash we can call back Buddy Brathwaite's bare, rat-proof feet, or Ginny Sukoloski's dungaree nipping duck, or Joey Lapella's green teeth?*"

Did You Know?

- **The first 4 books that Jerry had written were never published.**
- **Jerry always has chick peas in his pocket, in case he wants a snack.**
- **Jerry's first book for children was published when he was 41 years old.**

NAME: _____

Chapters One to Four

Part A

Answer the questions in complete sentences.

1. *Loser* is the story of a young boy who is quite unusual in many ways. Have you ever known a boy or girl who had trouble fitting in with other kids? How was this person different?

    _____

    _____

2. What advantages and disadvantages might there be in having such a person in your class at school?

    _____

    _____

Vocabulary

Choose a word from the list that means the same or nearly the same as the underlined word.

heedless	trolley	annoy	unpredictable	quiver
agreeable	instinct	sift	remarkable	constraints

1. There were <u>limits</u> placed on the children in the playground.

2. She had an <u>inborn ability</u> of knowing the right thing to say in all situations.

3. Gretzky was an <u>extraordinary</u> hockey player.

4. Zinkoff's lower lip began to <u>tremble</u>.

5. The movie's ending <u>could not be determined in advance</u>.

6. The <u>streetcar</u> runs right by my friend's home.

7. That loud noise is beginning to <u>anger</u> me.

8. The cook used a sieve to <u>separate out</u> the bugs from the flour.

9. The puppy was <u>unmindful</u> of his mother's warning bark.

10. The climate in California was most <u>suitable</u> to the early pioneers.

Chapters One to Four

Part A

1. Put a check mark (✔) next to the answer that is most correct.

a) Zinkoff's family live ten miles from a city of:

- ○ **A** one-half million
- ○ **B** one million
- ○ **C** two million
- ○ **D** five million

b) Zinkoff loved to:

- ○ **A** swim
- ○ **B** play floor hockey
- ○ **C** run
- ○ **D** play checkers

c) When the kids' mothers told them to stay off the streets, they took over the:

- ○ **A** sidewalks
- ○ **B** alleys
- ○ **C** parks
- ○ **D** back yards

d) In Chapter 3 the author refers to Zinkoff and his friends as:

- ○ **A** lemmings
- ○ **B** cubs
- ○ **C** brats
- ○ **D** pups

e) Zinkoff's teacher's name was:

- ○ **A** Miss Meeks
- ○ **B** Mrs. Kennedy
- ○ **C** Miss Marsh
- ○ **D** Mrs. Houston

Chapters One to Four

Part B

Answer the questions in complete sentences.

1. What do we learn of Zinkoff in the first chapter?

_____

_____

2. Describe how Zinkoff reacts to his new freedom in Chapter 2.

_____

_____

3. What does the author mean by the term "sidewalk pups" at the beginning of Chapter 3?

_____

_____

4. In Chapter 3 the author lists a number of contests that the "sidewalk pups" engage in. Can you think of two more contests that might have appealed to them?

_____

_____

5. Zinkoff hasn't yet noticed that he never wins any of the contests. What does this tell you about his personality?

_____

_____

Journal Activity

In the first three chapters, Zinkoff has not yet started school. Think back to when you were too young to attend school. Describe one interesting incident that happened to you when you were that age. You might describe an adventure you had or an interesting person you met.

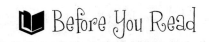
Chapters Five to Seven

Part A

1. Interview three of your classmates and ask the question, "What do you think are three important characteristics found in most good teachers?" Compile your results and list the top three responses below.

_____

_____

2. Zinkoff wears an unusual-looking giraffe hat to school. What might be the consequences for such a decision? Why?

_____

_____

3. Zinkoff learns a lot about the uniqueness and power of words in these chapters. Several of the words he meets are "made-up words or phrases". "Tintinnabulation." Is it a real word? If so what does it mean?

_____

_____

4. "He knocks over his desk with a **nerve-slapping** racket" (p.17) Nerves can't really be "slapped", can they? Yet why is this still a catchy expression?

_____

_____

5. What do you think the following expression might mean: "hitched a ride on a pencil point" (p. 18)?

_____

_____

6. The author does not spend a great deal of time describing Donald Zinkoff's appearance. In fact we don't really know the color of his hair, eyes, or even his skin - whether he's tall, short, fat or thin. On a separate sheet of paper draw a picture as to how you perceive Zinkoff to look.

Chapters Five to Seven

Part B

Word List

acorn
adventure
declared
direct
directly
drill
fascinate
forbid
forever
fork
gallop
grade
grade
head

legible
Meeks
perfect
picks
pt
realize
represents
retread
ribs
sad
silly
squad
tickle
Zinkoff

Across

1. To push forcefully.
5. Donald _____.
7. Fruit of the oak tree.
10. Is a symbol of.
12. A form of practice.
13. An exciting undertaking.
14. Donald was in _____ one.
16. Short for Play Time.
17. Miss _____.
21. To be aware of.
23. Donald tripped and _____.
24. Without delay or hesitation.
25. Donald was never _____.

Down

1. Touch lightly.
2. To be in charge of (as in films).
3. Prohibit or veto.
4. Clear handwriting.
6. Captivate with awe.
8. Remold (as in a tire).
9. Time without end.
11. A team.
14. Stated.
15. Something a horse will do.
16. Not even one mistake.
18. Goofy.
19. Chooses
20. Above the neck is one's _____.
21. A cut of meat (as in beef)
22. You eat with a knife, spoon and _____.

Chapters Five to Seven

Part A

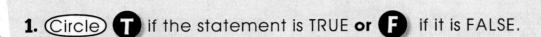

1. Circle **T** if the statement is TRUE **or** **F** if it is FALSE.

   T   F   **a)** Zinkoff's teacher addressed her class on the first day as "young citizens".

   T   F   **b)** The students were informed that there were 25,000 days before graduation.

   T   F   **c)** Miss Meeks pretended she was a pilot aboard the Learning Plane.

   T   F   **d)** Zinkoff's penmanship was superb.

   T   F   **e)** Zinkoff's family car was dubbed *Clunker Four*.

   T   F   **f)** Nothing tickled Zinkoff more than a funny word.

2. Number the events from **1** to **6** in the order they occurred in these chapters.

_____ **a)** Zinkoff shows his teacher how he can write his name.

_____ **b)** Zinkoff goes into hysterics over the word *Jibip*.

_____ **c)** Miss Meeks gives her opening day speech.

_____ **d)** Zinkoff has to wear a button which says, "I know I can behave"..

_____ **e)** The giraffe hat is a big hit at recess.

_____ **f)** Zinkoff's mother gives him a silver star.

NAME: _____

Chapters Five to Seven

| Part B | Answer the questions in complete sentences. |

1. What is your impression of the teacher's speech on Zinkoff's first day of school? Defend your answer.

_____

_____

2. Why do you think the author calls the main character by his last name throughout the novel?

_____

_____

3. Why was Zinkoff's teacher concerned about his penmanship?

_____

_____

4. Describe how the tall, red-haired boy's teasing backfired on him. How does he save face?

_____

_____

5. Where does Zinkoff think his mother gets the stars she gives him?

_____

_____

6. What "tickles" Zinkoff more than anything else? Give an example of this from Chapter 7.

_____

_____

Journal Activity

Miss Meeks' idea of making Zinkoff wear the "I know I can behave" button is one strategy she employs to make him control his behavior in class. Think of other effective strategies she might have used.

Chapters Eight and Nine

Part A

1. In these chapters, Zinkoff's new friend, Andrew, is upset because his family moved to a new house. What would be one advantage and one disadvantage to moving into a new home?

_____
_____

2. Which sport do you enjoy participating in? Explain why this sport appeals to you.

_____
_____

3. How would you describe Zinkoff's self-image at this point in his life?

_____
_____

4. What are the major influences on his life?

_____
_____

5. How do you think Zinkoffs habit of mimicking other children might become a problem for him as he gets older?

_____
_____

6. Some people find it difficult to keep friends for very long. Do you think that friends should be friends for life? Explain your answer.

_____
_____

Chapters Eight and Nine

Part A

1. Fill in each blank with the correct word from the chapters.

a) The _____ was Zinkoff's favorite cookie.

b) Zinkoff was born with an upside-down _____ in his stomach.

c) Zinkoff's soccer team was called the _____.

d) Zinkoff's nickname in Chapter 9 was _____.

e) At the end of Chapter 9, Zinkoff is sad because soccer season was

_____ .

2. Use the words in the box to answer each question.

mailbag	trophy	losing	stars	cookie

_____ **a)** Zinkoff was surprised to see two of these on the baby's diaper.

_____ **b)** Andrew is angry with Zinkoff for dropping this on the floor.

_____ **c)** Zinkoff threw up into this.

_____ **d)** In order to become better at this, Zinkoff practices for several weeks in the backyard.

_____ **e)** What did Zinkoff give Andrew after the soccer game?

NAME: _____

Chapters Eight and Nine

Part B

Answer the questions in complete sentences.

1. What two new friends did Zinkoff make during the summer after Grade One?

_____

_____

2. Describe Zinkoff's *snickerdoodle* strategy that he used to win Andrew's friendship. What caused the strategy to fail?

_____

_____

3. What particular physical problem did Zinkoff have?

_____

_____

4. Why did the game of soccer appeal to Zinkoff?

_____

_____

5. Why do you think Zinkoff felt it was important to be a "poor loser" in Chapter 9?

_____

_____

6. What generous offer did Zinkoff make after his soccer team won the championship?

_____

_____

Journal Activity

Zinkoff's favorite cookie is the *snickerdoodle*. **Research a recipe of _your_ favorite cookie. Include the recipe and give your cookie an unusual, personalized name. If you feel really creative, come up with your own cookie recipe!**

NAME: _____

Chapters Ten and Eleven

Part A

Answer the questions in complete sentences.

1. The title of Chapter 10 is quite interesting. What does atrocious mean? Predict what this chapter might be about.

_____

_____

2. Zinkoff's father is a mailman. On a separate sheet of paper design the following: an interesting mailbox to put in front of your house. Make it reflect something important about your personality or something you really enjoy (i.e. a picture of your favorite animal).

Vocabulary

Synonyms are words with similar meanings. Use the context of the sentences below to help you choose the best synonym for the <u>underlined</u> word in each sentence. If you cannot determine the meaning from the context, consult a dictionary.

1. Mrs. Biswell found Zinkoff's behavior to be insulting and <u>disrespectful</u>.

a) silly **b)** rude **c)** humorous **d)** noisy

2. Zinkoff's handwriting was <u>atrocious</u>.

a) stylish **b)** neat **c)** old-fashioned **d)** dreadful

3. The teacher grew tired of the boy's <u>antics</u> in the cafeteria.

a) pranks **b)** speeches **c)** charades **d)** stale lunches

4. Donald expects to drive a <u>respectable</u> distance.

a) short **b)** far **c)** good **d)** bumpy

5. Mr. Zinkoff is determined to make the day live up to his son's <u>expectations</u>.

a) goals **b)** anticipations **c)** hobbies **d)** riddles

Chapters Ten and Eleven

Part A

1. **Complete the paragraph by filling in each blank with the correct word from the chapters.**

On his first day of school in grade two, Zinkoff asks how many _____ of
a
school were left until _____. His new teacher's name was _____.
b   c
He also got into trouble on the playground by _____. His new teacher did not
d
like _____, and she hardly ever _____. The one thing that upset her
e   f
the most was _____. The teacher got _____ to help Zinkoff with his
g   h
penmanship. Zinkoff was always volunteering to answer _____. For every one
i
that he got right, he got _____ wrong. Zinkoff ruined his teacher's beloved
j
_____ by throwing up on it. After screaming at Zinkoff, his teacher was scolded
k
by the _____ in his office. She then bought Zinkoff a yellow _____ to
l   m
throw up in.

2. **Which word or phrase best describes:**

a) Zinkoff went to work with his dad on:
- ○ **A** Easter Monday
- ○ **B** Sunday
- ○ **C** Saturday
- ○ **D** Friday after school

b) Zinkoff's dad tells him to act:
- ○ **A** professional and friendly
- ○ **B** casual and interested
- ○ **C** stressed
- ○ **D** like he's having a good time

c) Zinkoff and Andrew's dad's were:
- ○ **A** janitor and attorney
- ○ **B** mailman and salesman
- ○ **C** salesman and bus driver
- ○ **D** mailman and banker

d) Zinkoff's workday was interrupted by:
- ○ **A** a rainstorm
- ○ **B** lunchtime
- ○ **C** a fire
- ○ **D** the car over-heating

Chapters Ten and Eleven

Part B

Answer the questions in complete sentences.

1. Describe how Zinkoff gets off on the wrong foot with Mrs. Biswell.

_____

_____

2. Why is laughter such a problem for Zinkoff?

_____

_____

3. Why is it strange that Mrs. Biswell is a teacher? Why do you think she chose this profession?

_____

_____

4. Why do you think Zinkoff's father congratulates him when he tells him his handwriting is *atrocious*?

_____

_____

5. Describe the events leading up to Mrs. Biswell's eraser being ruined.

_____

_____

6. How did Zinkoff's father manage to take him to work on his mail route, even though it was against regulations?

_____

Journal Activity **What do you think of the author's title for Chapter 10 - "Atrocious"? What does this title bring to mind?**

Chapters Twelve to Fourteen

Part A

Answer the questions in complete sentences.

1. Being a mailman is an interesting job. If you have the opportunity, ask a mail carrier what they find most interesting about their occupation. Think of two things about this occupation that would make it rewarding.

   _____

   _____

2. What would there be about delivering mail that might prove challenging?

   _____

   _____

Vocabulary **Choose a word from the list to complete each definition.**

convalescing	descending	contrary	critical	distinct
solitary	reassures	urgent	immense	coarse

1. A person who is alone is _____.

2. A voice which is very plain and clear is _____.

3. A surface that is rough to the touch is _____.

4. Something that is important is _____.

5. Someone going down is said to be _____.

6. A person recovering from an illness is said to be _____.

7. Something that is very large is said to be _____.

8. A person who is disagreeable is said to be _____.

9. A teacher who is constantly finding fault is _____.

10. A person who gives confidence to someone _____ that person.

Chapters Twelve to Fourteen

Part A

Put a check mark (✔) next to the answer that is most correct.

1. **Zinkoff's dad said that delivering mail in a storm was:**

○ **A**   a piece of cake
○ **B**   easy as pie
○ **C**   great fun
○ **D**   quite a chore

2. **The Waiting Man was waiting for:**

○ **A**   his mail
○ **B**   his brother
○ **C**   a parcel
○ **D**   the doctor

3. **Zinkoff delivered:**

○ **A**   25 letters
○ **B**   50 letters
○ **C**   75 letters
○ **D**   100 letters

4. **Zinkoff hates this more than anything else:**

○ **A**   school
○ **B**   broccoli
○ **C**   waiting
○ **D**   Polly

5. **Zinkoff's strategy in conquering the Furnace Monster was:**

○ **A**   a three day plan
○ **B**   a complete failure
○ **C**   a week-long plan
○ **D**   spoiled by Polly

   Loser CC2511

Chapters Twelve to Fourteen

Part B

Answer the questions in complete sentences.

1. What things does Zinkoff's father suggest they do on their lunch break?

_____

_____

2. Besides bad weather, list two other things Mr. Zinkoff suggested a mailman had to worry about?

_____

_____

3. What was unusual about *The Waiting Man*?

_____

_____

4. Why was the start of Third Grade the worst period of Zinkoff's life?

_____

_____

5. Why did Uncle Stanley call Zinkoff "The Sleepless Wonder"?

_____

_____

Journal Activity

Write a **TRIANGLE POEM** about being a <u>mail carrier.</u> A triangle poem has five lines and gets its name from the shape of the poem.
This is the pattern: Line 1 - title
Line 2 - two "*smell*" words
Line 3 - three "*touch*" words
Line 4 - four "*sight*" words
Line 5 - five "*sound*" words.
(Lines 2-5 all refer to the title.)

Chapters Fifteen to Seventeen

Part A

Answer the questions in complete sentences.

1. Do you think Zinkoff's *discovery* by the other kids will be a good thing or a bad thing for him? Explain your answer.

_____

_____

2. Describe how you might feel if everyone in your class started putting you down by calling you a cruel name. Why do you think this would have such an effect on you?

_____

_____

Vocabulary

A synonym is a word or word phrase that means the same as another. For example:

calm = peaceful   cry = weep   brave = courageous

Below are partial sentences taken from Chapters 15 - 17. Replace the underlined words in each sentence with a synonym. Use a dictionary or a thesaurus to find your words. Place the new word on the blank after the word phrase.

1. He is forever making <u>pronouncements</u> . . .

_____

2. Mr. Yalowitz notes his <u>atrocious</u> handwriting . . .

_____

3. Every Friday at <u>precisely</u> two thirty . . .

_____

4. . . . even an <u>incredible</u> final leg by Hobin is not enough . . .

_____

5. . . . six of the Purples have no <u>intention</u> of allowing Zinkoff to compete.

_____

6. So <u>fierce</u> is the Waiting Man's concentration . . .

_____

NAME: _____

Chapters Fifteen to Seventeen

Part A

1. **Circle** **T** if the statement is TRUE **or** **F** if it is FALSE.

T   F   **a)** The author refers to little-kid eyes as scoopers and big-kid eyes as *picky*.

T   F   **b)** Field Day for the little kids (grades 1 – 3) was all about races.

T   F   **c)** Mr. Yalowitz referred to the other grade four class and their teacher as measles.

T   F   **d)** The coach had Zinkoff run anchor in the final race

T   F   **e)** Thanks to his efforts during Field Day, Zinkoff's reputation was greatly enhanced in the eyes of his classmates.

2. Number the events from **1** to **6** in the order they occurred in the chapters.

_____   **a)** Zinkoff gets a bike which he calls Clinker One.

_____   **b)** Zinkoff's dad takes him for a ride in Clunker Six.

_____   **c)** Zinkoff is placed in seat number one at the front of the classroom by Mr. Yalowitz.

_____   **d)** Zinkoff meets Claudia, the little girl on a leash.

_____   **e)** At the Field Day, Zinkoff ends up on the Purples.

_____   **f)** Zinkoff begins grade five and is renamed.

Chapters Fifteen to Seventeen

Part B   Answer the questions in complete sentences.

1. Chapter 16 is in some ways the most important Chapter in this novel. Why do you think this is true?

   _____

   _____

2. Why do you think Zinkoff's teacher made Donald run anchor in the big race?

   _____

   _____

3. How did the following people react to Zinkoff losing the race: Zinkoff, Hoben, Zinkoff's dad?

   _____

   _____

4. What does Zinkoff realize about how his dad feels toward him at the end of Chapter 16? How do you know that?

   _____

   _____

5. What was so special about Grade Five at Satterfield Elementary?

   _____

   _____

6. How was Zinkoff renamed at the start of fifth grade?

   _____

   _____

What does the term "unconditional love" mean? Is this a valuable thing for a parent to practice? When a parent practices "unconditional love" consistently with their children, what advantage might these children have as they grow up?

Chapters Eighteen to Twenty

Part A

Answer the questions in complete sentences.

1. Think of one advantage and one disadvantage to having a *best friend*.

    _____

    _____

2. Interview a classmate and find out from that person the two characteristics they feel are most important in "choosing" a best friend.

    _____

    _____

Vocabulary

Circle the correct word that matches the meaning of the underlined word.

1. Binns is the most interesting person Zinkoff knows, with the possible <u>exception</u> of The Waiting Man.

    a) wonderful   **b)** exclusion   **c)** terrible   **d)** beautiful

2. The union will <u>negotiate</u> a new contract with the company.

    a) discuss   **b)** pick up   **c)** carry   **d)** party

3. <u>Ultimately</u> Zinkoff walked all the way to Willow Street.

    a) angrily   **b)** first   **c)** patiently   **d)** finally

4. A yellow cat, <u>emerging</u> from an air duct, studies him for a moment.

    a) crawling   **b)** racing   **c)** coming out of   **d)** breathing

5. He had the <u>impression</u> he could teach her to speak.

    a) feeling   **b)** dream   **c)** habit   **d)** talent

After You Read

Chapters Eighteen to Twenty

Part A

1. Fill in each blank with the correct word from the chapters.

a) Zinkoff put _____ Binns' name on the test, stating that he was his best friend.

b) Binns put _____ down on the test as his best friend.

c) Binns also collected earwax to make a _____.

d) Zinkoff got his first A on a major test in _____ .

e) Zinkoff hoped his pink _____ stone would bring him luck.

f) Zinkoff lived on the 900 block of _____.

2. Use the words in the box to answer each question.

Hobin	Yellow	licorice	Zinc	earwax

_____ **a)** After getting an A on his test, the other kids called him by this nickname.

_____ **b)** What team was Zinkoff put on for Field Day in grade 5?

_____ **c)** Who was also on the team?

_____ **d)** What did Zinkoff present to Binns which was in an Altoid can?

_____ **e)** What did Binns enjoy eating?

NAME: _____

Chapters Eighteen to Twenty

Part B   Answer the questions in complete sentences.

1.   What do you think are important criteria in determining a "best friend"?

_____

_____

2.   Why do you think it was so important for Zinkoff to have a best friend at this point in his life?

_____

_____

3.   Zinkoff has "bitter sweet" remembrances when thinking of his friendship with Binns. Explain the meaning of "bittersweet" in this context.

_____

_____

4.   Who did Zinkoff desperately want Binns to see on their walk?

_____

_____

5.   What happened when Binns slept over that ruined the experience for Zinkoff?

_____

_____

6.   What was Zinkoff's strategy come Field Day?

_____

_____

Journal Activity   Write a short biography of a personal "best friend" (past or present). Describe this friend's appearance as well as personality. Accompany your biography with an accurate sketch of your subject.

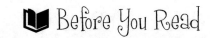

Chapters Twenty-one to Twenty-three

Part A

Answer the questions in complete sentences.

1. Predict what difficulties you think Zinkoff might experience when he transfers from his old school to a school for the middle grades.

_____

_____

2. Have you ever been faced with a very unpleasant experience that you somehow found a way of avoiding? Describe the experience. How did this strategy make you feel afterward?

_____

_____

Vocabulary

Write a sentence using the following words. Make sure that the meaning of each word is clear in your sentence.

a) deliberate _____

b) grimace _____

c) transparent _____

d) divert _____

e) astonish _____

f) citation _____

g) galore _____

h) boisterous _____

i) tofu _____

NAME: _____

Chapters Twenty-one to Twenty-three

Part A

1. **Complete the paragraph by filling in each blank with the correct word from the chapters.**

When the old lady asked Zinkoff what he wanted, he said _____. When

she said she didn't have any, he said he'd have a _____ instead. When Zinkoff
                                                          b

tells her he once got an A on a test, she says _____ and later gives him a
                                                          c

_____ sticker. The next day he found out that the _____ Team won
          d   e

the Field Day.

At graduation Zinkoff played the flute in the _____ . Katie _____
                                                         f   g

won a book for having the best grades. During the graduation's final number, Zinkoff

began to _____. When he was called to accept his graduation diploma,
              h

_____ shouts "Go Donald", and _____ gives him two thumbs up.
          i   j

For most of July, Zinkoff goes _____ crazy, carrying it with him wherever
                                         k

he went. His new school was called _____ Middle School, and there he
                                              l

discovered that the band had become the _____ band.
                                                    m

2. **Put a check mark (✔) next to the answer that is most correct.**

a) Andrew changed his name to:

- ○ **A** Drew
- ○ **B** Andy
- ○ **C** Andre
- ○ **D** Daniel

b) The only club Zinkoff didn't quit was:

- ○ **A** Camera Club
- ○ **B** Video Club
- ○ **C** Model Car Club
- ○ **D** Library Helpers

c) At Middle School Zinkoff comes to love:

- ○ **A** baseball
- ○ **B** football
- ○ **C** basketball
- ○ **D** ice hockey

d) At his new school he becomes less than a loser, he becomes:

- ○ **A** hopelessly careless
- ○ **B** a nobody
- ○ **C** surly and irritable
- ○ **D** very confused

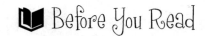 Before You Read

Chapters Twenty-one to Twenty-three

Part A   Answer the questions in complete sentences.

1.   What is Zinkoff's favorite sandwich? What kind did the old lady offer him?

_____

_____

2.   How is the old lady similar in appearance to a white mouse?

_____

_____

3.   Why do you think Zinkoff wants the old lady to continue calling him "Oh mailman"?

_____

_____

4.   What was the result of Zinkoff telling the old lady the stories from his life?

_____

_____

5.   What does Zinkoff worry about while he is waiting to get his diploma?

_____

_____

6.   How do Polly and Mr. Yalowitz support Zinkoff when he gets his diploma?

_____

_____

 **Journal Activity**

Write a HAIKU POEM about one of the following topics:
• **old people** • **summer holidays** • **graduation** • **marching bands**
• **pick-up games**

A Haiku Poem does not rhyme.
Line 1 has 5 syllables
Line 2 has 7 syllables
Line 3 has 5 syllables

i.e. The sport of brave kings
Long ago when knights jousted
Swords shone in the sun.

Chapters Twenty-four to Twenty-six

Part B

Answer the questions in complete sentences.

1. Describe what you like best about winter.

_____

_____

2. In your own words describe what **bravery** is. Give an example from your own experiences which illustrates **bravery**.

_____

_____

Vocabulary

In each of the following sets of words, <u>underline</u> the one word which does not belong. Then write a sentence explaining why it does not fit.

1.	fringe	edge	flounce	border
2.	fragments	pieces	portions	cereals
3.	cluster	lively	bunches	groups
4.	angered	petrified	stone-like	stiffened
5.	necessary	needy	plank	required
6.	silhouettes	shadows	profiles	statues
7.	utterly	justly	entirely	completely

NAME: _____

Chapters Twenty-four to Twenty-six

Part A

Put a check mark (✔) next to the answer that is most correct.

1. **Just before Zinkoff learned that Claudia had wandered off, what activity was he involved in?**

- ◯ **A** a street hockey game
- ◯ **B** building a snow fort
- ◯ **C** throwing snowballs
- ◯ **D** shoveling the Waiting Man's driveway

2. **According to Zinkoff, what flies truer than a snowball?**

- ◯ **A** a slushball
- ◯ **B** an icicle
- ◯ **C** an iceball
- ◯ **D** a snowball mixed with stones

3. **Where does Zinkoff decide to look for Claudia?:**

- ◯ **A** the park
- ◯ **B** the Waiting Man's backyard
- ◯ **C** the schoolyard
- ◯ **D** the alley

4. **What did Zinkoff keep in his hand for luck?**

- ◯ **A** his lucky rabbit's foot
- ◯ **B** his lucky stone
- ◯ **C** his medal from Field Day
- ◯ **D** Polly's lucky silver dollar

5. **When Polly ran away she made it all the way to:**

- ◯ **A** Zinkoff's school
- ◯ **B** Willow Street
- ◯ **C** Ludlow Avenue
- ◯ **D** Cleveland

NAME: _____

Chapters Twenty-four to Twenty-six

Part B   Answer the questions in complete sentences.

1. Why were the students so happy to see the snow?

   _____

   _____

2. What crisis visited the people of Willow Street?

   _____

   _____

3. Why does Zinkoff almost panic and try to stop the snow plow?

   _____

   _____

4. Why does Zinkoff "know" that Claudia is in the alley?

   _____

   _____

5. His pockets feel the same as his hands, cold and wet." How did that happen?"
   How did Zinkoff get soaking wet?

   _____

   _____

6. How did Zinkoff's father say that he was going to call Polly's bluff?

   _____

   _____

Journal Activity

Discuss Zinkoff's parents' strategy in allowing Polly to run away from home. Was this wise?

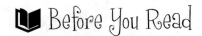

Chapters Twenty-seven to Thirty

Part A

Answer the questions in complete sentences.

1. Chapter 26 ends as a **cliffhanger**. What do we mean by this term? Why is it often an effective device that authors use?

_____

_____

2. Readers often appreciate a book with a happy ending. How would you end this novel on a *happy* note?

_____

_____

Vocabulary

Choose a word from the list that means the same as the underlined word.

spiral	canopy	dislodged	slogged
stashed	gaped	trance	balmy

1. The quarterback's tooth was <u>jarred</u> from his mouth.

2. The children <u>plodded</u> up the road to the cottage.

3. The old man <u>gawked</u> at the waitress in surprise.

4. The pirate <u>cached</u> the treasure in the oak tree.

5. The weather in Bermuda is often mild and <u>pleasant</u>.

6. The bridal party was covered by a <u>canvas covering</u>.

7. The whirlpool moved in a <u>circle</u>.

8. The witch cast a <u>spell</u> on the prince.

Chapters Twenty-seven to Thirty

Part A

1. **Circle** **T** if the statement is TRUE **or** **F** if it is FALSE.

T   F   **a)** Zinkoff was so tired that he fell asleep while he was walking.

T   F   **b)** Zinkoff was so cold that his teeth chattered.

T   F   **c)** Claudia was found in someone's back yard building a snow fort.

T   F   **d)** Zinkoff had been out all night and was found at six the next morning.

T   F   **e)** After his ordeal, Zinkoff still wanted to go play at Halftank Hill.

T   F   **f)** Zinkoff returns to school a great hero and no one ever picks on him or laughs at him again.

2. Number the events from **1** to **6** in the order they occurred in these chapters.

_____ **a)** Someone finds Zinkoff and takes him home.

_____ **b)** Zinkoff wakes up at three in the afternoon.

_____ **c)** Bonce picks Zinkoff for his team.

_____ **d)** Zinkoff imagines taking a nice hot bath.

_____ **e)** Zinkoff walks into a garage door and falls down.

_____ **f)** Zinkoff imagines Claudia's mother waiting for her daughter to return just like the Waiting Man.

After You Read

Chapters Twenty-seven to Thirty

Part B   **Answer the questions in complete sentences.**

1. Jimmy wonders if the Waiting Man ever thought of going to Vietnam and looking for his brother himself. Discuss the pros and cons of this idea.

_____

_____

2. Why do you think Zinkoff's <u>lucky stone</u> is so important to him after the Claudia incident?

_____

_____

3. What did Zinkoff feel happened when someone else touched his lucky stone?

_____

_____

4. Describe how Claudia's mother reacted when she first met Zinkoff after his ordeal.

_____

_____

5. Why do you think it is so important that Zinkoff is chosen in the last scene of the novel?

_____

_____

6. What do you think the last sentence of the novel "And let the game begin" means?

_____

_____

Journal Activity   **Toward the end of Zinkoff's ordeal, he becomes incoherent. Have you (or a friend) ever had an experience like this where you were at the very end of your strength?**

Chapters 1 to 4

Clever Ways of Saying Things

Jerry Spinelli is a very good writer who sometimes says things in unusual ways. Often the reader has to stop and think about what Spinelli has written.

Choose three of the following phrases and put them in your own words:

- *this brick and hoagie town (p. 3)*
- *the let-loose sidewalk pups (p. 5)*
- *tries to outstare the sun (p.3)*
- *the never-blinking sun (p. 4)*
- *as surely as noses drip downward (p. 5)*
- *the usually hatted students (p.9)*

Now think of three additional sayings that are unusual yet imaginative. They may be sayings you have heard or read – or ones that you just made up. Be sure to put the meanings to these sayings beside each one.

Chapters 5 to 9

Expressing One's Mind

Zinkoff learns a lot about the uniqueness and power of words in these chapters. Several of the words he meets are "made-up words or phrases".

- *"Tintinnabulation." Is it a real word? If so what does it mean?*
- *"He knocks over his desk with a <u>nerve-slapping</u> racket" (p.17) Nerves can't really be "slapped", can they? Yet why is this still a catchy expression?*
- *What did Zinkoff's teacher mean by the expression, "hitched a ride on a pencil point" (p.18)?*
- *When does Mrs. Meeks use the word "Jabip"?*

Now think of three additional sayings that are unusual yet imaginative. They may be sayings you have heard or read – or ones that you just made up. Be sure to put the meanings to these sayings beside each one.

Chapters 10 to 14

The Simile

The author enjoys using similes in this novel. A simile is a figure of speech showing a comparison or likeness of one idea to another by using the words "like" or "as". (i.e. He was as fast as a rocket.) Listed below are several similes the author uses in this novel. Explain what the writer is expressing and what two ideas are being compared.

- *His letters swarm willy-nilly across the page like ants on a sidewalk.*
- *His arms whirl like his mother's Mixmaster.*
- *He discovers her skin is almost transparent, like thin ice over a December puddle*

Now invent your own similes comparing the following items (remember to use *like* or *as*):

  a) *A hot day to the Sahara desert*
  b) *Chocolate birthday cake to (your choice).*
  c) *A little girl's smile to (your choice)*
  d) *(Your choice) (your choice).*

📝 Writing Task # 4

Chapters 15 to 20

An anagram is a word that is formed by changing the order of the letters of another word. For example, the letters in the word NAIL can also form the word LAIN.

Follow these directions to form the anagrams: a) Read the clue in the right-hand column. b) Using the word in the left-hand column - move the letters around in any order but you must use all the letters.

Word	Anagram	Clue
NOT		A large weight
TWO		To pull a car
STAB		The bills in a restaurant
STARE		Estimates the value of something
NOW		Opposite of lose
RACE		An anxious feeling

📓 Writing Task # 5

Chapters 21 to 23

COMIC BOOK HEROES

This activity is especially for students with an artistic flair or who love comic books!

It can be done for Chapters 21 - 23, or include events from Chapter 1 to 23.

> **The first step is to decide on the length of your comic strip (6 to 12 frames is suggested); next consider what events you will include. The student may wish to highlight a brief incident (i.e. Zinkoff's adventures delivering mail) or encompass the entire novel to this point. You may even want to provide an alternate ending to your scene!**

A quick sketch of the comic strip can first be accomplished in a storyboard format before a final, good copy is attempted. The strip should include a title, dialog, and color. It should be neat and imaginative.

- -

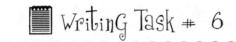

📓 Writing Task # 6

Chapters 24 to 30

Final Analysis

What did you like best about the novel "Loser"? What do you think the "theme" or main idea of the novel was? Be sure to include all the important details that made you like it.

How would you rate this novel?	____ Excellent!
	____ Great
	____ OK - I Can Live With It
	____ Not Too Good
	____ Downright Lousy

Why did you choose the rating you did?

NAME: _____

Word Search

Find the following key words from the story. The words are written horizontally, vertically, diagonally and some are even backwards.

absolutely	etiquette	medal	random
announces	haphazard	miraculously	serious
acquires	impressed	misinformed	Snickerdoodles
atwitter	intends	pacifier	soccer
Biswell	jabip	Polly	Vietnam
blizzard	mailman	quilted	Zinkoff

z	x	v	m	z	s	e	r	i	u	q	c	a	b	i	a
m	d	m	a	i	l	m	a	n	c	v	t	m	d	m	t
i	f	h	n	n	r	a	n	d	o	m	i	e	r	p	w
r	g	a	t	k	r	a	f	g	h	s	s	d	a	r	i
a	h	p	e	o	t	f	n	e	i	g	d	a	z	e	t
c	j	h	i	f	y	g	g	n	s	f	n	l	z	s	t
u	k	a	v	f	u	h	f	e	o	k	e	e	i	s	e
l	s	z	w	s	i	o	e	r	t	u	t	r	l	e	r
o	u	a	q	d	r	p	o	l	l	y	n	t	b	d	l
u	o	r	a	m	j	a	b	i	p	v	i	c	i	o	l
s	i	d	e	t	l	i	u	q	s	o	c	c	e	r	e
l	r	d	s	r	e	i	f	i	c	a	p	u	i	s	w
y	e	a	b	s	o	l	u	t	e	l	y	c	v	b	s
a	s	e	l	d	o	o	d	r	e	k	c	i	n	s	i
e	t	i	q	u	e	t	t	e	z	x	c	v	b	n	b

Comprehension Quiz

Answer each question in a complete sentence.

1. What was Zinkoff's teacher's name in grade one, and what did she call the students of her class?

_____

_____

2. Describe the hat that Zinkoff wore on the first day of school.

_____

_____

3. During the summer between grades one and two, two new people enter Zinkoff's life. Who were they?

_____

_____

4. What was the name of Zinkoff's favorite cookie?

_____

_____

5. What was Zinkoff's favorite sport when he was in grade two?

_____

_____

6. Describe what happened to Mrs. Biswell's beloved greenboard eraser.

_____

_____

SUBTOTAL: /12

Comprehension Quiz

7. What had happened to the Waiting Man's brother?

_____

_____   **2**

8. What test did Zinkoff give himself that took place in the basement of his house?

_____

_____   **2**

9. Describe one hobby that Hector Binns had that was rather odd.

_____

_____   **2**

10. What kind of a friend did Andrew (Drew) turn out to be?

_____

_____   **2**

11. What happened to little Claudia that caused all the excitement on Willow Street?

_____

_____   **2**

12. Describe Zinkoff's role in this little adventure.

_____

_____   **2**

13. How did the novel's concluding scene show that Zinkoff had made some progress since starting school?

_____

_____   **2**

SUBTOTAL: **/14**

   Loser CC2511

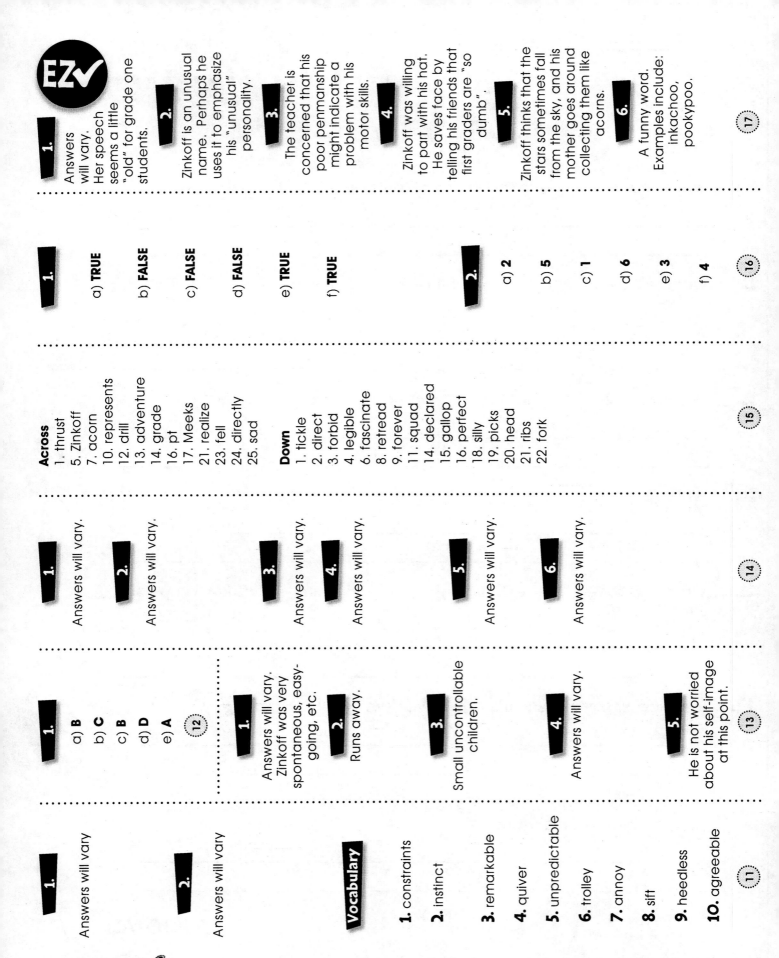

EZ✔

1. Answers will vary. Her speech seems a little "old" for grade one students.

2. Zinkoff is an unusual name. Perhaps he uses it to emphasize his "unusual" personality.

3. The teacher is concerned that his poor penmanship might indicate a problem with his motor skills.

4. Zinkoff was willing to part with his hat. He saves face by telling his friends that first graders are "so dumb".

5. Zinkoff thinks that the stars sometimes fall from the sky, and his mother goes around collecting them like acorns.

6. A funny word. Examples include: inkachoo, pookypoo.

(17)

1.
a) **TRUE**
b) **FALSE**
c) **FALSE**
d) **FALSE**
e) **TRUE**
f) **TRUE**

2.
a) **2**
b) **5**
c) **1**
d) **6**
e) **3**
f) **4**

(16)

Across
1. thrust
5. Zinkoff
7. acorn
10. represents
12. drill
13. adventure
14. grade
16. pt
17. Meeks
21. realize
23. fell
24. directly
25. sad

Down
1. tickle
2. direct
3. forbid
4. legible
6. fascinate
8. retread
9. forever
11. squad
14. declared
15. gallop
16. perfect
18. silly
19. picks
20. head
21. ribs
22. fork

(15)

---

1. Answers will vary.

2. Answers will vary.

3. Answers will vary.

4. Answers will vary.

5. Answers will vary.

6. Answers will vary.

(14)

1.
a) **B**
b) **C**
c) **B**
d) **D**
e) **A**

(12)

1. Answers will vary. Zinkoff was very spontaneous, easy-going, etc.

2. Runs away.

3. Small uncontrollable children.

4. Answers will vary.

5. He is not worried about his self-image at this point.

(13)

---

1. Answers will vary

2. Answers will vary

Vocabulary
1. constraints
2. instinct
3. remarkable
4. quiver
5. unpredictable
6. trolley
7. annoy
8. sift
9. heedless
10. agreeable

(11)

Page 18

1. Answers will vary.
2. Answers will vary.
3. Positive.
4. His parents, close friends, teacher.
5. Answers will vary.
6. Answers will vary.

Page 19

1.
a) snickerdoodle
b) valve
c) Titans
d) Wild Foot
e) over

2.
a) stars
b) cookie
c) mailbag
d) losing
e) trophy

Page 20

1. His baby sister, Polly, and his neighbor, Andrew.
2. He thinks that Andrew will have to come out and see the snickerdoodle he bakes.
3. Zinkoff was born with an upside-down valve in his stomach which causes him to throw up several times a week.
4. Soccer is free-for-all, where Zinkoff gets to run around.
5. Answers will vary. Perhaps he thought it was expected that he be like the other players.
6. He offered Andrew his trophy.

Page 21

1. Answers will vary.
2. Answers will vary.

Vocabulary

1. b
2. d
3. a
4. c
5. b

Page 22

1.
a) after
b) graduation
c) Miss Biswell
d) laughing
e) children
f) smiled
g) sloppiness
h) Andrew
i) questions
j) five
k) eraser
l) principal
m) bucket

2.
a) B
b) A
c) D
d) B

Page 23

1. Zinkoff asks the teacher how many days of school are left.
2. Zinkoff cannot control his laughter and is always laughing at inappropriate times.
3. Mrs. Biswell does not seem to like children. Answers will vary.
4. Answers will vary. Perhaps to keep his spirits up.
5. Zinkoff throws up on the eraser and ruins it.
6. He took him on Sunday when there was no official mail delivery.

EZ✓

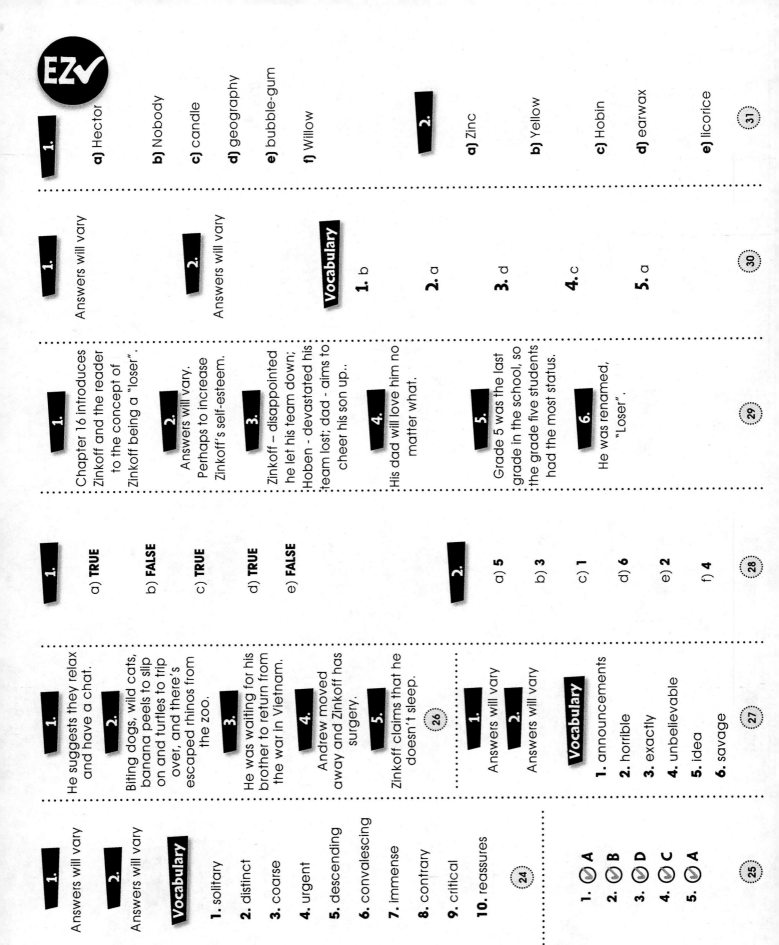

EZ✓

1.
a) Hector
b) Nobody
c) candle
d) geography
e) bubble-gum
f) Willow

2.
a) Zinc
b) Yellow
c) Hobin
d) earwax
e) licorice

31

---

1. Answers will vary

2. Answers will vary

Vocabulary
1. b
2. a
3. d
4. c
5. a

30

---

1. Chapter 16 introduces Zinkoff and the reader to the concept of Zinkoff being a "loser".

2. Answers will vary. Perhaps to increase Zinkoff's self-esteem.

3. Zinkoff – disappointed he let his team down; Hoben - devastated his team lost; dad - aims to cheer his son up..

4. His dad will love him no matter what.

5. Grade 5 was the last grade in the school, so the grade five students had the most status.

6. He was renamed, "Loser".

29

1.
a) **TRUE**
b) **FALSE**
c) **TRUE**
d) **TRUE**
e) **FALSE**

2.
a) **5**
b) **3**
c) **1**
d) **6**
e) **2**
f) **4**

28

---

1. He suggests they relax and have a chat.

2. Biting dogs, wild cats, banana peels to slip on and turtles to trip over, and there's escaped rhinos from the zoo.

3. He was waiting for his brother to return from the war in Vietnam.

4. Andrew moved away and Zinkoff has surgery.

5. Zinkoff claims that he doesn't sleep.

26

1. Answers will vary

2. Answers will vary

Vocabulary
1. announcements
2. horrible
3. exactly
4. unbelievable
5. idea
6. savage

27

---

1. Answers will vary

2. Answers will vary

Vocabulary
1. solitary
2. distinct
3. coarse
4. urgent
5. descending
6. convalescing
7. immense
8. contrary
9. critical
10. reassures

24

1. A
2. B
3. D
4. C
5. A

25

1. Answers will vary.

2. Answers will vary. Perhaps because he saw others with best friends.

3. Mixture of good and bad memories.

4. The "Oh Mailman" lady.

5. Binns was a restless sleeper.

6. He thought he would excel through practice.

(32)

---

1. Answers will vary.

2. Answers will vary.

Vocabulary

Answers will vary.

(33)

1.
a) snicker-doodle
b) sandwich
c) congratulations
d) turkey
e) Yellows
f) orchestra
g) Snelsen
h) cry
i) Polly
j) Mr Yalowitz
k) Monopoly
l) Monroe
m) marching

2.
a) Ⓐ A   b) Ⓓ D
c) Ⓒ C   d) Ⓑ B

(34)

---

1. pepper and egg.

2. Her skin color is pale like a white mouse, as well she has a pink scalp and pink eyelids.

3. Answers will vary. Perhaps it makes him feel important.

4. He feels much better.

5. He worries that no one will cheer him when he gets his diploma.

6. Polly yelled, "Go Donald! Go Donald!" and Mr. Yalowitz gave him two thumbs -up.

(35)

---

1. Answers will vary

2. Answers will vary

Vocabulary

Reasons will vary.

1. flounce
2. cereals
3. lively
4. angered
5. plank
6. statues
7. justly

(36)

a) Ⓒ C   b) Ⓐ A
c) Ⓓ D   d) Ⓑ B
e) Ⓒ C

(37)

---

1. They thought school might be cancelled because of a "snow day".

2. The little girl, Claudia, wandered away from home and couldn't be found.

3. He thinks the plow may run her over.

4. Answers will vary. Perhaps it is wishful thinking on his part.

5. Zinkoff has fallen a few times, plus it had been snowing quite hard.

6. He said he was going to let her run away and not try to stop her.

(38)

---

1. Answers will vary

2. Answers will vary

Vocabulary

1. dislodged
2. slogged
3. gaped
4. stashed
5. balmy
6. canopy
7. spiral
8. trance

(39)

1.
a) **TRUE**
b) **TRUE**
c) **FALSE**
d) **FALSE**
e) **TRUE**
f) **FALSE**

2.
a) **4**
b) **5**
c) **6**
d) **1**
e) **3**
f) **2**

(40)

Word Search Answers

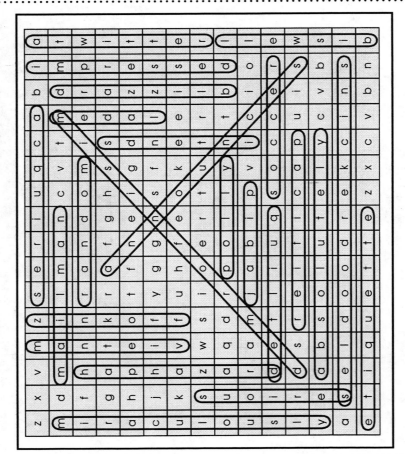

7.
He didn't return from the Vietnam War.

8.
Stay in the dark basement until he counted to 100.

9.
He was collecting earwax to make a candle.

10.
Fickle

11.
She wandered off and was lost.

12.
He spent seven hours searching for her in a snowstorm.

13.
He waited out the team captains and was picked for basketball.

47

1.
Miss Meeks.

2.
Big giraffe hat.

3.
His sister, Polly, and his friend, Andrew.

4.
Snicker-doodle

5.
Soccer

6.
He threw up on it after she yelled at him.

46

45

1.
Answers will vary. Probably too many years have gone by.

2.
Answers will vary. Perhaps because it was an experience they "shared".

3.
It lost its power.

4.
She was over-whelmed with emotion (very grateful)

5.
It was a small victory for him, and shows the reader that he is making headway.

6.
Answers will vary.

41